I dedicate this book to the everyday people. The teachers, the salespeople, the engineers, the plumbers - all those who work hard for their money. I hope this book helps you venture out with some of your investing dollars and enjoy the wild ride of the startup world.

The Everyday Startup Investor

THE EVERYDAY STARTUP INVESTOR

How Regular Folks Can Invest in Startups and Create Prosperity

BY TODD E. MCWHIRTER

Printed in the United States of America

First Printing, 2020

ISBN-13: 978-1-949001-47-1 print edition
ISBN-13: 978-1-949001-48-8 ebook edition

Waterside Productions
2055 Oxford Ave
Cardiff, CA 92007
www.waterside.com

Table of Contents

Introduction

Why Should Silicon Valley Have All the Fun?

Like a lot of people, you might be constantly investigating and researching the best way to get a return on your investment dollars. We all know that bank accounts barely offer any interest, so we divvy up our investments into real estate, stocks, bonds, mutual funds, ETFs, annuities, gold, silver, bitcoin, and other vehicles.

The question I have is this: Why do so few people consider startups as part of their strategy?

The common assumption has always been that the startup game is for Sharks on the ABC show or the venture capitalists from Silicon Valley who are trying to fund the next Facebook, Twitter or Snapchat — and that the rest of us are just spectators who maybe get to buy a handful of these exciting stocks when and if these companies go public years later.

This isn't true anymore. When the JOBS Act (Title III) opened up opportunities for un-accredited, everyday folks to invest in startups, the world changed. Along with other investments, I believe startups should be a small part of any investment portfolio. However, the average, everyday investor is often unaware of the opportunities out there, and might not know how to analyze a startup investment opportunity if it were available.

I stumbled into the world of startups 22 years ago. It wasn't exactly pretty at first. Some did well. Some failed. I made my first million at the age of 37, lost it all and declared bankruptcy in my mid 40s, yet made it back three times by age 53. Over the years, I learned from both my successes and mistakes, developing some pretty sensible ground rules for evaluating startup opportunities. These ground rules have helped me generate an average 7X return on all my startup investments and, equally important, it has been interesting, challenging and fun being a part of these early-stage ventures.

I can almost guarantee you that there is somebody living within a mile of your house that has a business plan and no capital. By learning how to find and evaluate these opportunities, you cannot only help drive innovation and job growth, you might even significantly increase your net worth. After all, why should Silicon Valley have all the fun?

I wrote this book in an effort to capture the key lessons I learned the hard way about startups over more than 20 years. I share what I learned from my successes, but more importantly, from my failures. There are ideas in this book that can help anyone succeed in the world of startup investing, while avoiding many of the common pitfalls.

The pages that follow give you a no-nonsense way to evaluate potential startup investment opportunities: how to analyze them, how to gauge risks and upsides, when to jump in and when to run the other way. I also give you a few tips on finding these opportunities. I am confident that if you apply the information that follows, you will embark on an adventure that enriches you and those around you — in more ways than one.

Thanks for reading!

Todd E McWhirter
TheEverydayStartupInvestor.com

WARNING & DISCLOSURE: THIS BOOK IS MEANT TO BE AN OVERVIEW AND A STARTING POINT. I DO NOT CLAIM THAT THESE PAGES HAVE EVERYTHING YOU NEED TO EMBARK ON STARTUP INVESTING. THE JOBS ACT (TITLE III) IS COMPLICATED AND HAS MANY RULES THAT MUST BE FOLLOWED. PLEASE DO NOT INVEST IN ANY STARTUP WITHOUT CONSULTING YOUR ATTORNEY.

Chapter One
If 9 Out of 10 Fail*, Why Bother?

Things Have Changed

Believe it or not, for decades it was illegal for a startup company to solicit investment capital from a Regular Joe unless he was either a friend or family member. Government regulations decreed that the only people who could back a startup had to be "accredited investors" (sometimes called "sophisticated investors") — meaning they had to have a net worth of $1 million or income greater than $200,000/year. To be sure, there was a legitimate (but not necessarily right) argument for this: 9 out of 10 of these investments might fail. Uncle Sam couldn't let the Regular Joes take that kind of risk, seeing them as not wise or sophisticated enough to make their own decisions and determine for themselves the risks inherent in this exciting and potential wealth-building ride.

---

* *not meant to be an exact statistic, but rather a reminder of the high-risk nature of startup investing.*

Things have changed. With the JOBS Act (Title III), the average person can now invest. Although this legislation brings the most significant rule changes in nearly a century, plenty of requirements and restrictions remain. The JOBS Act is complicated and confusing, and even though you don't have to be accredited anymore, you need to know what you're doing, and you will need to consult an attorney. Although I feel that opening the gates was the right move, we also know that the risk of losing money with startups is still very real, and the odds are definitely stacked against you. Hence this book.

Crazy Gambling vs. Educated Gambling

Yes, 9 out of 10 might fail, but if you get sound legal advice and educate yourself, I believe the guidelines in these pages can help turn what would otherwise be crazy gambling into a more viable high-risk/high-reward investing strategy – what I like to call educated gambling.

To increase the odds in your favor, you will need to:

1. Learn how to manage your money so that you are only investing money you can lose.
2. Develop an analysis framework for evaluating:
    a. The odds of success for an entrepreneur's idea.
    b. The management team's skills and likelihood for them to succeed at their roles.
    c. The valuation of the company, i.e., what are you actually getting for your money, and is it fair?

   d. The offering and the exit strategy — how are you going to realize return on your investment?
   e. The entrepreneur, their track record, their character and their abilities.
2. Get some tips for finding real investment opportunities.

How Much Should I Invest?

This number is up to you, **as long as you are following the guidelines in the JOBS Act**. However, the most important thing is that you don't let your emotions govern the way you arrive at this number. I can tell you from experience that emotional investing is the fastest way to lose money.

Start by picking an amount you are willing to lose. Then pick an amount that you can repeat at least 10 times over 10 years, because in my experience, you need at least 10 of them in your portfolio to give you enough diversity for this type of investing. A good rule of thumb is to never invest more than 5-10% of your total *investing dollars* into startups. Only invest "play money" that you're willing to lose, and have fun doing it.

Many of the startups that you will find out there will have $25,000 to $50,000 minimums, but with the Jobs Act there are opportunities developing for investors at the $2,000 to $5,000 levels. Some invest a *small* portion of their IRA money using a self-directed IRA custodian (*small* meaning an amount you don't need to retire on).

Others save a little each month in a "startup jar" fund. Some join with others and invest as a group to hit certain minimums. There are many ways to make this work, but to repeat, the most important startup investing rule is to invest with logic, not emotions, and invest only what you are willing to lose.

The Buck Stops with You

Although this book will be a guideline to help reduce your risk, let it be known that investing in startup companies is for people who take 100% responsibility for their decisions. The *Decision Buck,* so to speak, stops with You and You alone. This is high-risk investing. You will lose money with many of your investments. You will miss out on some that could have made you millions. My hope and goal is that you will experience a handsome return on your money in the long run, and I do believe these strategies will increase the odds of that actually happening.

However, the law of averages does not lie, and one rule of thumb is that dabbling is the surest way to lose money. That's why it's my belief that you should invest in a minimum of 10 startups to create proper diversity. All that being said, let me be very clear with this information:

1. You will pass on some startups that might have made you rich.
2. You will jump into some startups that will lose every dime you put in.

3. This is still basically educated gambling (yet still gambling) and is only for people who take 100% responsibility for their decisions.

If you fully understand these facts and are still ready to get involved in the startup world, please read on…

Chapter Two
The Idea

It's natural for the idea to be front and center during the initial conversation with an entrepreneur who is looking for money. This is one of the fun parts — listening to a passionate entrepreneur explain how their idea is going to be huge. Your job is to vet this idea, asking some basic questions and determining whether you believe this particular idea has the potential to make big money.

The first task is to get a clear understanding of the idea. Warren Buffet is known for this simple rule of thumb: "Never invest in a business you cannot understand." This may sound obvious, but it takes some inquiry to get to the core of most ideas. After you have a basic understanding of the idea, you must dig deeper. You need to find out what problem this idea is solving:

1. What need or problem is the idea filling or solving? How vital is that need or problem?

2. Does this idea capitalize on a market shift — or could it just be a fad?
3. Does the idea create loyalty, or put another way, does the idea have "stickiness?"
4. What are competitors doing in this space and how is this idea different from them?
5. How easy would it be for other players to become competition? What are the barriers to entry?
6. Has the idea been tested?
7. Can the idea scale, and to what level? What market segment does the idea fit into and how big is that market? Do the costs decrease for producing the product or providing the service in greater volume?

Clear Understanding of the Idea

This sounds simple, right? You will be surprised at how fast an idea can get complicated:

- *Early in my investment career I backed a company called Zoom Culture. The idea hinged on the deployment of a website filled with videos uploaded by user contributors. Sounds a lot like YouTube, yes? And this was a good five years before YouTube. The problem wasn't the idea; the problem was no clear understanding of who the customer was and what problem the entrepreneurs were solving. To be fair, they were sitting on a billion-dollar idea – streaming videos online. But without a clear understanding of how this idea would be implemented, how it would bring in revenue and how it would scale, this idea never got off the ground.*

I remember asking questions about revenue and hearing about five or six different potential revenue scenarios. Given my limited experience, all these scenarios sounded great. Looking back, I understand how important it is for the entrepreneur to have one solid and tested revenue stream, a clear understanding of who their customer is and why their customer will buy this product or service.

Here is a list of questions that will help you determine whether the idea is clear and understandable:

1. What problem does this idea solve?
2. What is the mission statement of the company?
3. How does this product or service fulfill the mission statement?
4. What is the primary revenue stream?
5. Who is the target market?
6. Describe the idea as if you were in front of a 2nd grade classroom.

These questions should be easy to answer for the entrepreneur. If they are not easy to answer and if you can't understand very clearly how the company will make money and be embraced by the target audience, then you might be better served by passing on the opportunity.

<u>Know the Competition</u>

If an idea has any value, there's either already competition in some form, or competition is on its way. Competition is not necessarily bad or good. Competition, if understood and handled correctly, can actually make the company sharper, better and more profitable. Determining whether the entrepreneur has a good grip on the competitive landscape — and understanding clearly his/her plan to thrive in a competitive context — is your job.

- *I remember getting pitched on a company a few years ago. When I asked about the competition, the answers I got were vague. I got back to my office, did a little online research and found major competitors that were not mentioned verbally or in the business plan. Certainly, the founder of this company knew about these competitors. I figured he was either hiding them or didn't have a plan to beat them. Regardless, I did not invest.*

Here are a few conversational angles that will help you determine whether the entrepreneur knows the competition and has a winning plan to beat them:

1. Tell me about the competition.
2. Tell me who might become the competition if this takes off.
3. How is this different?
4. What is unique about this product or service?
5. How does the plan create loyalty?
6. Is the market big enough for multiple competitors?
7. What is the philosophy regarding competition?
8. What are the barriers to entry that competitors must overcome?

Their answers should be clear, passionate and baked into the strategic approach. Competition is either already entrenched or poised to appear.

Look for an entrepreneur that sees competition as a motivator for becoming more service-focused and creating better technology. As Peter Thiel coined so clearly in his book, *Zero to One,* look for an entrepreneur that is motivated to become 10 times better than the competition.

Has the Idea Been Tested?

If you have spent any time watching ABC's *Shark Tank,* you will understand this concept very well. During almost every show, this question is asked: "How many have you sold so far?" or, "how much revenue have you brought in so far?" What the Sharks are looking for, of course, is proof of concept in the form of dollars. Does the product or service actually sell, and if so, to what degree? Before you invest in any company, you must ask this question.

You will hear opportunities in many different stages. Your job is to assess the level of sales that makes sense based on where they are in the process.

You might catch the company after it's been in business for a year or so. They are making sales and doing well, and they are raising money to scale. If this is the case, then sales should be fairly significant. Raising money to scale, if sales are barely happening, is a red flag. You want to look for a sign that sales are not the problem. You want "good problems," such as the entrepreneur is seeking to raise more money to produce more because sales are happening, or to expand the market of a proven product. A company looking to add technology and systems to create efficiency and, therefore, generate more profit is an example of a "good problem."

You might hear a pitch from an entrepreneur who has yet to launch their company. They are raising the funds to launch, and if you ask the "revenue question" that the Sharks ask, it's unlikely you will get an answer that would win the Sharks' confidence. I would not necessarily run away from a company at this stage, because you will most likely get more equity for your money. I would, however, assess whether they have properly tested their sales process so you can determine whether there is a significant demand, whether it's priced correctly and whether the margins are great enough to create healthy profits.

Additionally, market tests have to be strong and credible indicators of market interest. Weak and non-credible product or service testing can be an expensive mistake.

Weak: I would hesitate to invest, for example, if the test for selling the product was an online survey offering potential consumers a chance to say "yes" or "no" to a "would I buy this product?" question.

Strong: I would more likely invest if the test was with a specific sample size and had click-through statistics — with a healthy portion of the sample size actually entering a credit card number to make a purchase. This is a demonstrable buying decision.

Here are some questions that will help you navigate this important piece of the puzzle:

1. How much of the product or service have you sold so far?
2. What is the company's average monthly revenue?
3. How do people purchase the product?
4. Tell me how the product or service has been tested in the marketplace.
5. What are the demographics of the customers?
6. How do you find customers?
7. What are the marketing channels available to reach those customers?
8. Is it relatively cost efficient to market to those customers?

Chapter Three
Can the Idea Scale?

I personally love Mom & Pop businesses. I frequent them often in my neighborhood and try to support them with my dollars. My investing dollars and purchasing dollars, however, are two very different things. When I look to invest, I am always asking the question: How can this business idea scale? Determining this is a function of how large the market category is and where the product fits in the category's lifecycle. Also imperative for scaling is the need for proper sales, marketing, technology and systems. (Another major factor for scaling a company is the skill set of the entrepreneur, which I will discuss in a later chapter.)

What Market Category Does the Idea Occupy?

The category in which the idea resides and where that category is in its lifecycle is possibly more important than the product itself. I will describe my investing statistics in a later chapter, but suffice it to say, most of my successful investments started with one product and, during the first few years of struggling to make the business work, the entrepreneurs discovered the *real* moneymaking idea and totally changed the product or service, yet stayed within the broader category. Having a product in a market category that has not peaked (but is on the rise) and a market category that is substantial in size or expanding rapidly, are definitely important factors you want to look for.

- *I almost invested in an idea called Smart Family Deals during the Groupon mania. Remember when Groupon was on the front page of every business magazine? Thankfully, I did not go forward with Smart Family Deals — not because it was a bad idea, but because it was in a category that had peaked and had nowhere to go but down.*
- *My second investment is also a great example of the importance of lifecycle. It was the late '90s and the product was a little plastic kit that you could use to professionally label your CDs (instead of using a marker). We caught this market category on the rise and rode the wave perfectly, then sold the product for a very big win. If we were three years later in that product category's cycle, we would have never made any money.*

Below are some points and questions you should ask an entrepreneur who wants your investment dollars:

1. Tell me about the business or market category that the product occupies.

2. What stage in the market category lifecycle is the product in? Please explain why.
3. Explain why this product is in its beginning stages? If not, help me understand why this is exciting.
4. How big is this category?
5. Explain why this category will continue to grow.
6. Where is the trend going and where does the product fit into that trend?
7. Can you show me how you know this?
8. Is there any research you can provide that demonstrates this is true?

Sales and Marketing

Scaling a business requires successful implementation of a detailed and organized sales and marketing plan. Of course, there are thousands of books on this topic, but for the scope of this book, I am going to focus on a few specific things to look for and some specific questions to ask so you can better determine whether the founder has a grasp on the subject.

Some of this will be covered in more detail in a later chapter, *Vetting the Entrepreneur.* First, let's cover some important things to look for in sales and marketing:

Sales:

1. It's great to see a founder who is willing spend at least 25% of their time selling.
2. Look for a low base pay and a good commission structure for the sales team. Good salespeople

should make plenty of money – possibly even more than executives who aren't selling anything. The margins of the product or service need to be healthy enough to afford a generous commission structure.

3. It's important to see if the sales team has an opportunity or will have the opportunity to become owners via an employee option pool. If not an option pool, make sure there is at least some sort of bonus or profit sharing.
4. Look for a good sales process. Does the sales team have a solid sales pitch and understand how to get past gatekeepers, how to find a need and close the deal?
5. Is there a sales software and customer relationship management (CRM) system that is already in place? Successful sales require proper follow-up, and there must be a system in place for this.
6. Is there a clear prospect list or a plan to create one? The team should know exactly who they are calling on and how to get to those people.
7. Look for a sales schedule: When are people making calls, when are they following up? Sales is hard, and without a strict schedule, most likely will fail.
8. The founder should understand the sales cycle. In other words, find a founder who understands that quality sales involve much more than just talking about how great the product or service is. Good sales must include finding the need, creating a buying atmosphere, answering objections and a good close. The sales cycle should also

build long-term relationships and have a system for gathering referrals.

9. The sales pitch must be an honest and not exaggerated. Cheap, overpromising sales approaches will always end badly.
10. Look for passion. Passion sells; it's important to see that the team believes wholeheartedly in what they are selling.
11. Is there a track record of success? Look for a sales team that has successful sales experience in their past.
12. Finally, as discussed earlier, it's imperative that the product or service is selling now or in the least has been successfully and accurately tested in the marketplace. The Sharks always ask (and you should, too), "how many have you sold so far? What are your average sales per month?"

Marketing:

1. Look for a founder who has a grasp of marketing in the Digital Age – somebody who has knowledge of both content marketing and social media — and a believable plan to effectively and affordably leverage them (see more below in "Technology and Systems").
2. Is there a healthy, accurate and realistic marketing budget? The founder should be able to explain the dollar costs that specifically gain awareness, create prospects, and convert to sales. If your

entrepreneur simply tells you that, "we're going to put up a Facebook page," or "we're going to go viral," be skeptical!

3. It's important to see a detailed marketing plan — one that demonstrates that the founder understands how the sales team and the marketing plan work together. One that touches customers and potential customers differently and with different frequency based on where they are in the buying journey.

Technology and Systems

I touched on this in the section above, but it's worth repeating: Investors should be looking for an entrepreneur who demonstrates an ability to test, evaluate and leverage social media, marketing technology and content strategy in a cost-effective way. There are dozens of strategies — and even more tools, channels and platforms — for attaining the awareness and conversion gains your entrepreneur needs to deliver. It's *imperative* that the entrepreneur has a handle on this.

Rather than get bogged down in a tactical discussion here, I just want to underline that any entrepreneur worth their salt will have a detailed and defensible plan for bringing in leads that grow the company. A lack of detail in this area is a *major* red flag. While you won't always have the expertise to question the legitimacy of each tactic or tool, you can and should expect a numbers-driven strategic starting point — including how they plan to scale, test and improve their marketing ideas.

We all know what it's like to experience inefficiencies: A task that should take five minutes takes 20 minutes because we don't have a system in place. Scaling a business from the "Mom & Pop" stage to something that makes shareholders wealthy takes a leader who understands and can implement systems that create efficiencies in every area of the business. Creating systems in every area of the business takes a leader who can employ the latest technologies to create these systems.

I have been known to say that every company these days must become a "tech company" for me to invest. Below are examples of three different investments I have made that certainly would not have been considered "tech companies," yet each uses the latest technology to create winning systems and efficiencies:

- *The workspace company that I recently invested in has a training room that needs to be rented out often — or else it gets turned into offices. The question I had was this: "What is your sales and marketing plan for keeping the training room full?"*

  The answer I received was exactly what I had hoped to hear: They planned on spending some money on search engine marketing. When people need a training room in Denver, many will simply Google "training rooms in Denver" or "conference rooms Denver." Using search engine technology, they are able to target people looking for exactly what they are selling, bringing in revenue well above the marketing costs, creating happy customers and increasing shareholders' wealth. They also plan on narrowing this type of marketing. There are certain types of industries that use training rooms more than others, and by using technology, they can be found by these niche groups simply by having an ad pop up online, at the right time, targeted to the right type of audience.

- *When I was analyzing a liquor store business, one efficiency strategy being used by the entrepreneur was a digital pricing system. Think of how much time it takes for employees to put paper price tags on bottles of wine or on the shelf below the cases of beer. Imagine a scenario where the business needs to move particular products to maintain proper inventory levels. With a digital pricing system, this can be done with a mouse and a click. This is a classic example of a leader using technology to create efficiencies that add more wealth to the bottom line over time.*
- *Another example is a company I have been invested in for years – they do ground transportation for wealthy customers and recently invested in the creation of an app to solve the common problem of clients' flights landing early or late. The only way to make sure that the client and driver did not have to wait around was through a string of emails, texts or phone calls. Their app solved this by having all parties involved be able to access and enter any changes in the travel plans. This eliminated the need for the emails, texts or phone calls, saved time and money, created a better and more secure experience for their clients — and, therefore, more wealth for shareholders.*

Below are a few questions that will help you discover if the founder has a grasp on proper technology and systems:

1. Tell me about the marketing plan. Who is the audience and how do you plan on getting your message to them?
2. Tell me about the follow-up plan. How does your marketing accommodate different stages of a potential customer's interest level?
3. How do you plan on using social media, search engine marketing and content marketing strategies?
4. Help me understand the marketing budget. How much will it cost to get a new lead? A new customer? What is your approximate return on investment (ROI) on marketing dollars spent?
5. Is there an app in your future? If so, what problem would it solve?
6. Help me understand your plan to scale the business.
7. Where are the inefficiencies in the business and how do you plan on implementing systems for more efficiency?

Chapter Four
Ideas are a Dime a Dozen

You can take the title of this chapter literally. This means 10 cents buys 12 ideas, which makes the idea (no matter how great) worth less than one penny. If you're an entrepreneur yourself, you may totally disagree. The entrepreneur *knows* that their idea is worth millions. But let me approach this from the investor's perspective.

How many of us have sat in a bar somewhere and had an amazing idea that we knew would make us millions? The bar napkin was filled with drawings and outlines. You leave the bar excited and ready for the next step. But the next step never happened. Why? Because proper execution and implementation are a thousand times harder than thinking up good ideas. This is probably the most important point in this book: When we invest in a startup business, we are not betting on the idea nearly as much as we are betting on the entrepreneur to successfully implement and execute the idea – or, more likely, a *derivative* of the original idea.

We are investing in a *person*, not an idea. We are ultimately betting on the ability, skills, attitude and character of the entrepreneur, not their business plan, product or service.

Patents, copyrights and other product/service features do have value and are important to the equation, but in my humble opinion, the skills and character of the entrepreneur are vastly more important. I have seen and experienced great ideas from not-so-great entrepreneurs that went south, and I have seen mediocre ideas flourish in the hands of great entrepreneurs.

So, while we analyze the idea using the information in the previous chapters, we must always be asking ourselves the more important question: Do I believe this entrepreneur has the skills and character to succeed through a good economy or a bad economy? Character, good or questionable, might reveal itself as their plan for using investor money unfolds, how they approach valuation or their willingness to implement a profit-sharing plan or an employee option pool. Skills, good or questionable, could show up when we analyze things like their marketing and sales plan, the reality of their exit strategy or the management team they have built.

An analysis of my investment track record — and the different types of entrepreneurs I have backed — will shed some light on why I think the way I do and why I believe this extra focus on the entrepreneur's skills and character is the correct approach for analyzing startups.

I have invested in 39 companies over the last 22 years. Three have been homeruns; nine have made me good money. Another five broke even (I basically got my money back). Twelve have been total failures. The rest are still in business — most doing well, some struggling, but I have not seen a return yet.

I'm repeating, but it's that important: *The ability and character of the entrepreneur is far more important in making investors money than the idea itself.* Let me give you some statistics from my case files to back this point up: Out of the 12 companies that have made me good money (including the three homeruns), only six made me money with the original idea. Six of the 12 (and 100% of my homeruns!) had to dramatically change the idea and/or product/service once market feedback showed them new threats and opportunities.

Making this critical pivot relies a lot on the character and ability of the entrepreneur. Here are a few examples:

- *When I invested in Fortis Riders Corp., the idea originally pitched was a pre-paid taxi service for college kids. What it became was a company that provides high-end chauffeur service for wealthy business people. An entrepreneur without the ability to implement such a dramatic change of plan would never have succeeded. An entrepreneur of questionable character could have easily justified shutting down the pre-paid taxi business and relaunched the high-end idea without us.*
- *When I invested in MediaStore, Inc., the idea first pitched to me was an online store that would sell*

multiple storage solutions and other software products directly to customers. What made me the big money was one product that started to sell like crazy—the entrepreneur took that one product, created a separate "one product" company, and invited all of us original investors to come along at the same (extremely fair) valuation we got for the initial concept.

He then re-invented his own version of the product, used big box retailers to fill their sales funnel and wildly succeeded. This was a total change in both the product and the way the product was sold. A greedy entrepreneur could have let the original company die and started the new one without bringing us investors along. Or he could have valued the new company with a proven product so high that our ROI would have been nominal. An entrepreneur with questionable ability might not have seen or been able to pull off such a dramatic transformation of a business plan, which was paramount to the success of the venture.

- *US Americom was another company in which I invested and at the time, they sold copy machines. They now sell internet telephone solutions and are making headway again.*
- *Lewis and Clark, Inc. is a retail store similar to REI. As they ramped up the business, they discovered a type of sock that sold very well. They decided to develop their own sock company, make some improvements and develop the brand. To this day, the sock company has tremendous value for the company and hopefully for the shareholders down the road.*

Out of my 12 total losses, there is no question that at least 10 of these failures were not because the idea was bad, but because the entrepreneur running the show did not have either the character to protect their investors or the ability to adapt to the situation and navigate toward success.

- *While I was an investor in Zoom Culture, I watched the CEO at the time take $200K a year in salary for two years while the company slowly became worthless. Character shows its colors when times get tough.*
- *Smith Center, a hemp clothing company, was in 300+ retail stores when I invested. When they got into some cash flow issues (something all startups struggle with), they could have come clean, scaled back and survived the storm. Instead, they went full-throttle trying to raise more money based on false information in their investor presentation. By the time the investors and I found out, the company was already in the toilet.*
- *When I invested in a small telecom company called Vomerica, they had a deal on the table that would have made all of us investors a great return. Unfortunately, the deal fell apart, not because of a character flaw, but because the entrepreneur lacked the ability to navigate the situation and opportunity. This lack of ability cost me a good return.*
- *BullionReview was another company that failed, not because of character, but lack of proper focus. The company lacked a dedicated individual entrepreneur that*

> *served as a distraction-free driver of the business (which I will discuss later in the book). The result was failure.*

My hope is that with my real-life examples, you now understand that trying to figure out what startups to invest in is much more than just analyzing the product or service idea.

A thought I now know to be true – something I have learned through the years: "If the entrepreneur does not want to make you money, you definitely won't." That said, analyzing character is more of an art than a science, so use your gut! Analyzing skills is a little more straightforward, yet also can be challenging. Vetting the entrepreneur (and also the team) is your most important task, which we will cover in Chapters Seven and Eight.

Chapter Five
The Offering

The offering and the exit are like the front and back doors to your investment. You bring money and enter the business through the offering, and you hope to get your money — plus a handsome return — through the exit. Although I have divided the offering and exit into two chapters, it's very hard to separate the two, as they are intimately connected - one affects the other.

In this chapter, I will give you a high-level understanding of the types of offerings and entities — as well as some thoughts on valuation, warrants, preferred returns and share price.

Types of Offerings

The two types of offerings you will most likely see are a convertible note offering or a straight equity offering.

The *convertible note* is an investment strategy used by entrepreneurs who sometimes want to delay setting a valuation until a later (and usually much larger) round of funding — many times called the Series A round. This type of offering has become very popular, especially in the tech community. Essentially, the convertible note allows the entrepreneur to raise money at a future, unknown valuation. The entrepreneur borrows the money from investors (at, say, 10% APR), and when the company raises big money later, the loaned money (plus interest) converts automatically (or sometimes by investor choice) into equity at the valuation that is usually set by the bigger investor, or at a capped valuation agreed upon at the beginning of the deal.

Without some sweeteners thrown in, this type of deal is more advantageous for the entrepreneur than the investor. They get to use the investors' money to build their company, hoping to create a higher valuation. With a higher valuation, the investors' money buys less equity. We therefore experience less upside when the exit plays out. The interesting thing is that the loaned money is almost never collateralized — it has the same high downside risk as any other startup investment with an undetermined and vague upside. So why has this become popular? Who would do this?

I believe that the reason the convertible note has become popular in the tech community is because these entrepreneurs realize that they are going to need to raise millions of dollars, sometimes hundreds of millions, to reach their goal. If they set the valuation too early, the math just does not work. They would have to give up a large amount of the company for relatively few dollars brought in. When they later go for their Series A, they would then be diluted to the point of losing motivation. The convertible note solves this problem and allows the entrepreneurs to launch the company using borrowed money and set the valuation at a later date when they have a proven track record. They raise the big money to scale rather than launch, allowing them a much higher valuation and keeping a healthy amount of the company themselves, which motivates and inspires them for the difficult task ahead.

Although I do feel that the convertible note is often more advantageous for the entrepreneur, I understand it has its place and is often the logical way for entrepreneurs to set up their first offering. There are, however, some key points to understand before jumping into a convertible note offering.

1. Convertible notes, where investors have the choice to convert to equity, are sometimes pitched as lower risk because you, the investor, can eventually take your money back with interest and not convert to equity if you don't like the equity deal down the road. At some level this is true, but this also assumes they will get a deal down the road — that the big money will materialize and there will be a fair valuation to participate in *or* plenty of money to buy you out if you don't want to participate. If the big money does not come in the door, where will the company get the money to buy out all of the convertible notes? There usually is no collateral with these convertible notes. Although

this is a loan, and loans should carry less risk than equity purchases, investing in a convertible note is equally as risky as investing in a straight equity play.

2. The exit scenario upside must be tremendous because the equity your money buys will be at an undetermined and, most likely, very high valuation. To make the "ROI vs. risk" equation digestible, the upside must be realistic *and* hugely lucrative.
3. There should be incentives added in for convertible note investors: caps on the valuation and/or discounts locked in for the convertible note investors.
   a. Having a cap on the valuation takes some of the vagueness out of the equation for the investor. An example would be a cap, say at $2 million. In this scenario, even if the company were raising the big money at a $5 million valuation, the convertible note investor would convert to equity at a $2 million valuation ceiling. This allows the investor to do their due diligence with that cap in mind.
   b. Having a set discount on the future valuation is also a common incentive added to the convertible note document because it's fluid for the entrepreneur *and* more acceptable for the big money investors down the road. An example: the option to convert the note into equity at a 20% discount from the set valuation. Therefore,

if the valuation comes in at $5 million, the convertible note has the option to convert at a $4 million valuation.

c. It's best for the investor if the convertible note includes a cap and/or a discount, whichever is more favorable to the investor. Using the same numbers, this is where the note would convert to equity at the lesser of the $2 million cap or a 20% discount from the Series A round. Therefore, if the Series A came in at a $5 million valuation, the note would convert at the $2 million cap (since $2 million is less than 20% discount from $5 million). However, if the big money came in at a valuation of $2 million, the note would enjoy the 20% discount and convert at a $1.6 million valuation.

4. Convertible notes are usually written up by an attorney; therefore, it's important that you also have an attorney review the documents to make sure the legal paperwork and your understanding of the deal are equal. The devil is in the details, so things to look for are:
   a. What happens if the company sells before the money converts? Do you, the investor, get to enjoy the sale as if your money converted or does the company retain the right to merely pay back your principal and interest?

b. Do you have a choice to convert to equity or is it automatic? What happens if qualified financing (the big Series A) never comes to pass? Do you, the investor, have the choice to ask for your money back or is conversion to equity a requirement?
c. Beware of tax implications. The accrued interest you are "enjoying" is taxed as income even though it's merely "paper gains." Consult your accountant.
d. Obviously, you are looking for a convertible note that is "investor friendly." You won't necessarily get everything you want, but having your attorney explain the legal jargon to ensure you understand how the note plays out is important.

The *straight equity offering* is more straightforward: X dollars buys you Y percentage of the company. This is my preferred way of investing. One of the upsides in comparison with the convertible note is that you can do the math when you invest. (I will go into more detail later in this chapter under the section called "Valuation.") Generally, if you invest in a company with a million-dollar valuation, you need a $30 million sale of the company to get a 30X return. It's more complicated than this, of course, because there might be future rounds of investing that would dilute your percentage. But with the straight equity offer, you most certainly can get a better handle on the deal that is being offered.

A couple of important things to understand about straight equity offerings:

1. No matter how good the deal sounds, plan for future dilution. It's almost inevitable that the company will have to raise a second or even a third round of money, and although the goal is for those second and third valuations to be much higher (meaning less dilution), there is no guarantee of this.
2. Straight equity is what it is: Once you invest your money, most likely you are now a minority shareholder in a company and therefore have given up 'personal control' of your money. The upside can be ridiculous, but the downside is always a 100% loss of your investment.

Types of Entities

Most likely you will be investing in a C-corp, an S-corp or an LLC. It's important that you understand the pros and cons of each entity and the effect each could have on you — particularly in how you will be taxed.

S-corps and LLCs are taxed as flow-through entities. In other words, the company does not get taxed on any profit or get the benefit from any losses. All the tax issues flow straight through to the shareholders on a K-1 tax form. This can have a very real effect on your financial situation. If the company has a loss for a particular year, you as a shareholder then get to write off that loss *pro rata* on your taxes. If the company has a profitable year, you will have to pay taxes on that profit *pro rata.* Simple enough, right? There is, however, a catch. What if the LLC or S-corp decides *not* to distribute the profit to the shareholders, but rather keeps that profit in the company for future growth? Who, then, pays the taxes on the profit? Answer: The shareholders (you) would have to pay taxes on money never received.

Does this actually happen? If so, why would anyone invest in an LLC or an S-corp? The key to avoiding this situation is making sure that the operating agreement has a provision that prevents this – and making sure that this provision cannot be altered. Rarely will 100% of the profit be distributed, as the company will need to reinvest a portion of the profits to grow. But distributing at least enough to cover everyone's taxes is a must, and this provision must be in writing and any change must require a super-majority of shareholders votes, therefore, giving investors some control in this important area. Be sure to ask specifically — and double-check that the operating agreement clearly speaks to distributions in a way that protects the investor and cannot be changed by the founding team. Consult your attorney before you invest.

Another frustrating experience with LLCs or S-corps is the likelihood that you must delay your own taxes because the K-1 form for the entity you invested in did not get to you in time. Startup entrepreneurs wear many hats, are overworked and susceptible to some degree of chaos. Most of my LLC or S-corp investments have been late on their own taxes multiple times. If they are late on their own taxes, your taxes will be delayed. It's just the reality of the startup world. (I have become accustomed to filing for an extension on my taxes each year. This is not a big deal for me.)

Typically, this problem does not persist, but if this is a concern of yours, it's important to talk about this with the entrepreneur before you invest. One key to avoiding this is to make sure there is a "detail person" on the team. I will discuss this in more detail when we talk about the entrepreneur's team.

The C-corp, by contrast, is not a flow-through tax entity. The C-corp entity is taxed on its profits and gets to write off its losses without any effect on the shareholder. On the surface, this might sound like the preferred entity, but this kind of corporation has its downside, too. First, it's what is known as a *double taxed* entity. The company is taxed on profits before any distribution; if there is a dividend paid *or* a sale of the company, the shareholders get taxed on the money they receive as well.

In the end, more money as a percentage goes to Uncle Sam with C-corps than with S-corps or LLCs. Another nuance of the C-corp is the built-in lack of motivation to make a distribution to shareholders. The shareholders are not being affected by profits, so why not just keep all the profits in the company for future growth? This is normal if the exit plan is to sell the company, but it can be a frustrating experience to watch your investment make a profit year after year — long after the plan was to sell the company — yet no money flows through to the shareholders. I will share some ways to avoid this situation in later chapters (*Vetting the Entrepreneur* and *Vetting the Team*).

Valuation

The TV show *Shark Tank* has helped millions understand the basics of valuation. It's almost always the first thing that gets brought up during an episode. An entrepreneur says something like, "I am asking for $100,000 in exchange for 10% of my company." The Sharks reply with something like, "so you're telling me your company is worth $1 million. How much of your product have you sold so far?"

The term "valuation" can refer to either *pre-money valuation* or *post-money valuation.* The idea here is that the company is worth more after the money is raised than it is before the money is raised. Here's a simple formula to help you understand this:

Pre-money Valuation + Amount of money raised = Post-money Valuation

The *Shark Tank* example I used above is a post-money valuation because once the $100K is brought to the company, the Sharks get 10%, which would mean the post-money valuation is $1M. ($900K pre-money valuation + $100K = $1M post-money valuation.) The math adds up because $100K is 10% of $1M. For the sake of simplicity, I am going to use the term "valuation" interchangeably with "post-money valuation" because that is the way most entrepreneurs will present the offering. Most first-time entrepreneurs will say something like this: "I am valuating my company at $600K because I am raising $200K and selling 33.3% of the company." This is technically a post-money valuation, but what is more important than dickering about terminology is figuring out if what we are getting for our money is a good deal, a great deal or an awful deal.

Let's say you have $25K that you are hoping to invest in a startup company. In one scenario you get 2% of the company for the $25K and in another scenario you get 10%. In the first scenario you bought in at a $1,250,000 valuation; in the second scenario you bought in at a $250,000 valuation. Which is better? This is where separating the exit from the offering becomes impossible, because it really depends on several things, including risk level of the business, experience of the team, exit strategy potential and many other factors.

Let me give you some real-life examples to help you understand this:

> *Some time ago I invested in two different companies, one where $25K bought .05% of the company, representing a $5 million valuation, and another where $25K bought 5%, representing a $500K valuation.*
>
> *The first was a company with a seasoned entrepreneur who had a patent for his product process — and sales already in the millions and growing at a rapid pace. Their exit, if the team can succeed, is a sale somewhere between $50 and $100 million in three to five years, which would be a 10-20X return on my money. $5 million is an extremely high valuation for any startup, but when I considered the amount of sales already happening, the pace that they were growing, the track record of the entrepreneur, the team the entrepreneur had built and the likelihood of a sale in this industry, the valuation made sense.*

The second instance was with a couple of first-time entrepreneurs who have a small co-working space company. I invested in their second location because they have proven the model and the exit is dividend-driven. They set up the offering with a preferred return of 8% plus an accelerated principal payback. In other words, the investors were treated as if we owned more of the company than we did until we were made whole. The goal was to average 30% on our money each year, which is not a huge projected return in the startup world. But the fact that they had a proven track record, had an ideal location, had negotiated a 20-year lease and set things up with an accelerated principal payback all made a realistic exit and valuation picture for me.

These are clearly very different valuations and two very different investments, yet I jumped on both. Why? Because I believed the valuation made sense considering the potential of each exit. Keep in mind, I say "no" to many more investment opportunities than "yes." And when I say "no," it is often because the valuation does not make sense in light of the potential exit. Let me give you an example of this:

- *I was approached by a tech company who was trying to raise $2 million (with a $25K minimum from any investor) and selling 40% of the company, representing a $5 million valuation. The exit was a sale for $100 million or more. The category was quite intriguing, as it was in the real estate industry and had the potential to be as big as Zillow, which has a valuation* *in excess of $1 billion. The reasons I turned down the deal were many, but one of them was lack of sales. They had approximately $100,000 in sales and did not have a track record of repeat business. Although I still believe there is a chance that they could hit it big, the valuation and reality of their exit did not make sense considering the unproven track record, model and team.*

- *Another smaller-scale opportunity I passed on was in the fitness industry. They had a unique angle: To sell one membership that gave their customers access to multiple fitness centers. They were raising $300K and selling 30% of their company, representing a $1 million valuation. Although the business plan was intriguing and I thought it might succeed, their sales at the time they pitched me were very low, their track record was hard to determine, and the exit numbers were weak. They were hoping to sell the company for $5 million or start paying dividends — either way, the math did not add up. Although this is similar to the return I said "yes" to earlier – almost a 5X return (or 30% annual return) on investor money over a six-year period — when I looked at the likelihood of the exit and compared my risk to my potential return, it wasn't even close to what I would consider an acceptable offer. The valuation did not make sense in light of the exit.*

Warrants

Warrants are sweeteners sometimes added to the offering that, depending on the warrants and the success of the venture, can be very beneficial to the investor. They are basically stock options added to the deal. The warrants can range from "very exciting" to "not worth the paper they are written on." You might see something like this: If you invest $25K, then you will get a five-year option to invest another $12.5K at the same valuation. (This fits in the "very exciting" category.)

Or you might see something like this: If you invest $25K you will get a one-year option to invest another $25K at a later valuation set by the Board of Directors. (Not very exciting.)

The two important aspects to look for in an option are the amount of time you get to exercise the option and the valuation at which you get to exercise that option. Of course, the longer the time frame and the lower the valuation, the better the option.

Warrants are great incentives, and it can never hurt to ask for them if they are not offered already.

Preferred Returns

Like warrants, a preferred return is a sweetener that is sometimes a part of the offering. A preferred return strategy as part of an offering is a personal favorite of mine. It can limit the risk of our principal because the entire premise is that we investors get our money back in some sort of preferred way. There are many ways that preferred returns can be set up. Let me illustrate with a couple of real-life examples from my case files:

- *As mentioned before, one of my recent investments was a company that offered shared workspaces. They had a master lease on a piece of prime real estate that was perfect for creating a space to rent out to individuals and small companies. One of the founders is an architect, so the design came naturally and at a great price. Their plan was to pay dividends to the investors and give them 50% of the deal in exchange for their money. Then they added the sweetener: First, they had a guarantee of 8% APR on the invested money; second, they set it up so that the investors were treated as if we owned 75% of the deal until we got our invested principal back. As dividends start to flow, we will get a preferred return. Once we are made whole, we revert back to owning 50% of the deal. It's a win for everyone and most definitely something that helped me say "yes" to the offering.*

- *I once consulted with a startup whose exit plan was to sell the company, but they still eventually offered a preferred return. They were trying to raise $250K and offering 25% of the company. The goal was to sell the company for between $5-10M in three to five years. Doing the math, that is a possibility of a 5-10X investor return if everything goes as planned. Given the inherent risk of startups, they were having a tough time getting investors to open their checkbooks. I encouraged them to offer a preferred return. They set it up so the $250K initially invested indeed bought 25% of the company, but also sat on the books as an interest-free loan to be paid back first — before any profits were taken by the shareholders. However, they did not have to start paying down that note until year five. This way, if they met their goal and sold the*

> *company, the loan would get paid first and then the big payout would follow. If it took longer than five years to sell the company, then there were payments on the initial $250K over the next three years. It was a win for everyone involved and helped protect the investors' principal.*

Preferred returns can reduce the risk to the principal invested, and that is always a good thing for us investors. As with warrants, it can never hurt to ask for them — even if they are not in the original offering.

Share Price

Many times, you will hear the entrepreneur talk about the share price in the offering. *It's important that you are not fooled into thinking the share price has anything to do with the valuation.*

Let me explain: If Company X is selling their shares for $1 per share, Company Y is selling for 10 cents per share and Company Z is selling their shares for $50 per share, the natural thought is that Company Y is the cheapest and Company Z is the most expensive. This couldn't be further from the truth. Shares are nothing more than a "unit" that represents a percentage of the company. If, for example, the shares costing $50 per share came out of a pool of 10,000 outstanding shares, then $25,000 gets you 500 shares, which is 5% of the 10,000 shares outstanding. This gets you 5% of the company. Converting back to money, this represents a $500,000 valuation:

- $25,000 / $50 per share = 500 shares purchased
- 500 shares / 10,000 outstanding shares = .05 or 5%
- $25,000 invested / $500,000 valuation = .05 or 5%

On the other hand, if the company selling shares for 10 cents had 20 million shares outstanding, then the same $25,000 gets you 250,000 shares, which is 1.25% of the 20 million shares outstanding, therefore buying you 1.25% of the company. Converting back to money, this represents a $2,000,000 valuation:

- $25,000 / $.10 per share = 250,000 shares purchased
- 250,000 shares / 20,000,000 outstanding shares = .0125 or 1.25%
- $25,000 / $2,000,000 valuation = .0125 or 1.25%

It's a tricky little illusion that is easy to figure out once you know the right questions to ask and do some basic arithmetic.

The math doesn't have to get too complicated here. All you need to do is ask these questions: How many shares does $25,000 buy? Answer: 250,000 shares. OK, what percentage of the company will I own after I own 250,000 shares? Answer: 1.25%. OK, what then is your valuation?

If the entrepreneur has a hard time answering these basic questions, my suggestion is don't invest. They should know these numbers inside and out and their failure to do so would be a major red flag.

Chapter Six
The Exit

Back to the analogy: The offering is like the front door of your investment and the exit is like the back door. If you can't see a *clear, real and exciting* way out the back door, then you should never enter the front door.

Remember the premise that "9 Out of 10 Startups fail – Why Bother?" I am confident that the information in this book will increase these odds quite a bit, but your ROI in the startup world must have a much bigger upside than in typical investments because even the best startup analyst in the world will still have a good portion of their startup portfolio fail.

The reality is that you must make up for the failures with some pretty substantial returns on your winners. There is not an exact ROI that I can say I look for because it depends on many factors. Is there a preferred return? Is there a track record of sales and success? Are there any assets or intellectual property to sell if the company fails? How seasoned is the entrepreneur? A business plan with no revenue driven by a first-time entrepreneur, for example, would need to show a real possibility of a 50X ROI over a 7- to 10-year period for me to invest, as the risk is substantial. A proven model with a seasoned entrepreneur who has set up their offering with a preferred return for the investors might only need to show me a 6X ROI over a seven-year period, which is approximately 30% each year.

There are only four ways you can experience true ROI in a startup investment: dividends, a sale of the company, the company buying back its shares, or an Initial Public Offering (IPO – the company going public). I will cover each of these exit strategies over the next few pages, asking similar questions for each exit: Is the exit plan exciting enough for the risk? Is there a detailed and clear plan? And, is the exit based in reality?

Dividends

Dividends can be a very exciting exit. Cash flow is king, as they say. If you find an investment that can realistically distribute healthy dividends, it might be an opportunity worth investing in. Here are a few areas that need attention for a dividend exit to be taken seriously:

1. Study the profit margins. Healthy margins are key to profit and without a healthy profit, dividends will not happen.
2. Study the actual and pro forma financials. Are the expenses realistic? Are the expenses broken into detail so that you can better understand if they are accurate? Is the projected growth rate realistic? Are the profit projections realistic? If

you are not familiar with looking at financials, it would be a good idea for you to have them looked over by your CPA.

3. What are the projected dividends? Take that projected dividend number and cut it in half. Take the projected dividend time frame and double it. With these adjustments, how long will it take to recoup your investment? Is that adjusted projection still exciting? Is that worth the investment risk?
4. Does the entrepreneur have the skill set and character to build a team? You will hear this again in the next few chapters: It takes a team to build a company; it takes a leader to build a team. Look for competent team builders.
5. Does the entrepreneur want/need dividends to happen? I will cover this in more detail in the chapter called *Vetting the Entrepreneur*, but suffice it to say that you want the entrepreneur on the same page as you — getting wealthy through the exit, not through salary or unchecked bonuses.

Selling the Company

This is the most common exit I have seen in my investing career. With this exit an investor can become truly wealthy if things come together as planned. As with all the exits, however, you must analyze the details to determine the reality of the plan:

1. Study the actual and pro forma financials. As with the dividend exit, the actual financials and

the projected financials must be both detailed and realistic. Many times, you will see projections that grow revenue at a pace that is simply not realistic. Many times, you will see expense items that are vague and need to be broken out into detail. And again, run the numbers by your CPA if you are not familiar with looking at financials.

2. Is there a detailed plan in the foreseeable future for the sale of the company, or is the exit strategy nothing more than a vague comment like, "we're either going to sell the company or go public in three to five years."
3. With this exit, the entrepreneur should have comparable company sales for you to study – other, similar companies that were acquired by bigger companies. Find as much detail surrounding these acquisitions as possible. Were they cash sales? Stock sales? Did the acquisitions take place in a similar market to the one in which your entrepreneur will compete? Are they truly comparable or do you feel the entrepreneur is reaching a bit by using them? If the idea is truly original, are there *really* no comparables for you to consider? This is not necessarily a deal-breaker, but you should still look for comparables in the business category. In other words, if the idea is in the transportation industry, encourage the entrepreneur to find some company acquisitions in that general category.

4. Do the math and compare the valuation you are getting with the proposed exit sale. That number is your potential ROI. In other words, if you invest into a $500K valuation and the projected sale is $10 million in five years, your potential ROI is 20X in five years. Now adjust with a reality check: Cut that number in half and double the projected time frame. Given the startup risk, is the adjusted ROI still worth it? In this example, that would be 10 times your money in 10 years — about a 26% compounded yearly return. Is the risk worth this potential return?
5. What is the skill set of the entrepreneur and the team? Have they ever sold a company before? Do they have people on the board of directors who have done so? Always remember you are investing in people more than the idea or the plan.
6. Does the entrepreneur want/need the sale to happen? Do they have close friends and family in the deal that motivates them to achieve the exit? Are there salary caps in place for the founder that ensure the entrepreneur's wealth is created the same way as the investors'? I will cover this in more detail in the chapter called *Vetting the Entrepreneur*, but it's imperative that the entrepreneur is on the same page with the investors.

<u>The Company Buying Back Shares</u>

I am not going to spend much time on this exit as it only works well with niche-type investments where the risk is substantially less than your average startup. This exit would be plausible, for example, if the opportunity is buying into an apartment building with a seasoned developer where there is no bank involved.

At this point, the investors basically would have the building as collateral until they were paid out, so a much lower ROI would be required to attract investing dollars. The company, through later financing with a bank, would also have a clear way to provide a healthy return. Other than an investment with this type of collateral, I personally have never found this exit appealing for the following reasons:

1. The proposed ROI normally does not match the risk.
2. When I ask, “where are you going to get the money to buy back shares?”, I have never heard an answer that satisfied me. Even if the exit states that they will buy back your shares for a healthy 5X in two years, the question still lingers — where will they get the money to do that? What if they don’t? What is Plan B?
3. When a company is buying back shares, it’s usually because they see the future is bright compared to the buy-back price. There is a natural conflict of interest with this strategy that breaks the same page philosophy, which is paramount.

Going Public (IPO)

Going public is basically when a company sells shares of their stock to the public for the first time. It's when a private company becomes a public company.

There are three ways a company can go from a private company to a public company. One way to go public is simply to hire a lawyer and file all the paperwork with the Securities and Exchange Commission. If everything is in order, after a long process, the company can get a symbol on what's called the Pink Sheets, which is the lowest level of public companies. If this is the exit that is being pitched, I would personally stay away from this investment.

The second way to go public is to do a reverse merger. Basically, this is when a private company buys the majority of a public company's shares. Most of the time, what's being bought are "shells," meaning they do not have any real value except the fact that they are already public. The two companies then merge and now the private company is public. There are examples of success stories with this process, but if doing a reverse merger is the exit strategy, I would personally pass on the opportunity.

The third way, and the one you will most likely hear as an exit strategy, is what's called an Initial Public Offering. This is where the company hires an investment bank to go through the long process of taking the company's stock to the public at a specific offer price. Twitter (TWTR on the NYSE) is a successful example, as the company boasts a net worth in the billions.

IPOs as an exit strategy can be very exciting and make investors a healthy ROI, however, they are by far the most difficult exit to accomplish and typically the most expensive to execute (primarily due to legal costs and investment banking services required). Therefore, it's crucial to take the extra time and ask yourself the all-important questions:

1. Is there a detailed, clear plan?
2. Is the plan based in reality?
3. Has anyone on the founding team or the board of directors pulled off this type of exit in the past? Do you believe the entrepreneurial team has the skill sets and experience to succeed at this type of exit?
4. Does it make logical sense for this type of company to go public? In other words, would there be an extremely broad market opportunity for this type of company?
5. Is there a detailed plan for this exit or is it just a general statement like, "in five years we plan on going public?"
6. What is the market environment? IPOs usually happen when times are good, and the market is booming.
7. Study the actual and pro forma financials. As with the other exits, look for reality and detail. Broad and unrealistic revenue projections and expenses that are not broken out into detail should be considered red flags.

8. As with the other exits, you want to look for the same page philosophy. Are there checks and balances such as salary caps or close friends and family in the deal that make it imperative for the exit strategy to happen in a reasonable time frame?
9. Beware of broad statements like, "you are getting in at 10 cents per share and we are planning on going public at $2 a share." Although this sounds good, you need to understand that price of shares does not tell you much. You need to ask yourself what valuation you are buying into and at what valuation they plan on going public — *then* analyze the reality of this claim.
10. An IPO typically brings in many millions of new dollars, which dilute the stake of existing shareholders. This is not always a bad thing if the net worth of the company soars because of the demand, but it's important that the entrepreneur can speak to this and explain why this will ultimately be best for early investors.
11. Usually when a company goes public, the early investors are restricted from selling their shares for one year. This rule is in place to protect the new investors from buying in only to see the stock crash based on all the original investors cashing out. It makes sense, but keep in mind that this brings another layer of risk. During that year, many outside factors can impact the stock price, sometimes in a positive way and sometimes in a negative way.

12. In short, taking a company public through an IPO can be a very exciting exit. However, it is extremely difficult, is an arduous and very long process, has many new risks associated with it and requires a seasoned team to succeed. Taking the time to analyze the detail of the plan and the reality of the plan are more important than ever.

Chapter Seven
Vetting the Entrepreneur

One of my all-time favorite stories in my startup career was from early on. I call it the Mike Story and share if as often as I can with people.

- *It was my second investment with Mike Hummell and because the first one went well, I had brought many friends and family into this second investment. One of those investors was my litter sister Amy, who at the time was in her 20s and just out of college with her new job as a 2nd grade teacher (in other words, she was still broke). I was newly married at the time and was out of the country on an extensive traveling adventure – back-pack style for 16 months – and therefore off the grid and not accessible at the time.*

  Amy, fresh out of college, with a low-paying first teacher job started second-guessing the wisdom of investing her precious $1,000 (yes, that's not a typo: one thousand dollars). She got a hold of Mike and asked if *she could pull out of the investment – if he would be so kind as to buy her out and return her money.*

Mike was kind. So kind that 20 years later telling the story still triggers huge emotion. He sent Amy her $1,000 and told her that she still owned her stock. He explained that this was a loan back to her and that she could pay him back another time with no interest and no time frame. Nine or 10 months later, Amy received a check for $64,000 from the sale of the company.

Mike was working on the sale of the company when Amy requested him to buy her out. Honestly, I don't know many people that would have done what Mike did for my sister. It was over the top.

He could have been "kind" and had the company buy her shares back as Amy requested which would have benefited him the most. With a little legal work, he could have probably gotten his board to approve him buying her shares back himself and pocketing the full $64K.

Mike, however, is the kind of guy that gets excited about making his investors money, even the little investors. He loves having people in the boat with him and literally gets joy out of making people a great return. I have witnessed him giving his attorney and other people huge bonuses as gifts. Who does this sort of thing? Mike does.

The challenge with investing is that it's very hard to know what kind of person you are investing in. You don't need someone this generous to make good money, but you still need to determine the real (or not so real) desire for the entrepreneur to make you money. To repeat a saying I mentioned earlier, but something that from my experience has proved to be very true: *If the entrepreneur doesn't WANT to make you money, you definitely won't.*

Trying to determine an entrepreneur's character and skill set is always going to be subjective, but over the years I have used a few simple tests that will help you with this process. I am not saying that an entrepreneur has bad character if he or she doesn't pass these tests. Only the Great Spirit knows the heart. However, these tests have served me well in picking *winner investments*, which as I've discussed, is really picking *winner entrepreneurs.*

The overall feeling you get after talking with an entrepreneur is important. Does it feel like a poker game where you're adversaries who are each trying to win more than the other guy? Or does it feel like an engagement where if all goes well, you might end up in some sort of marriage characterized by transparency, honesty and being on the same team? What you are looking for is genuine transparency and a "Same Page Philosophy." Trust your gut!

The more you can find out about the founders' pasts, the better. The following tests are designed to help decipher whether an entrepreneur has the skills and character needed to wildly succeed. I also have laid out a few questions under each test to help get the process going. Follow up your questions with phrases like, "tell me more about that," and listen for hints and clues about skills and character that you can explore further.

Uncle Bob Test

Allow me to explain how this test came to be with a real-life story:

- *I was 99.9% ready to invest in a startup that had been pitched to me. This was going to be my third or fourth investment, so I was still fairly new to the game. Everything about the investment sounded perfect. He was a sharp guy who knew his stuff. I understood the business model and was convinced that this was going to be my next investment. Then I asked the question, the answer to which caused me to second-guess and eventually decline the opportunity.*

  I asked him who else had invested in his idea. Then I asked him if he had tried to raise money from his close friends and family. His answer was what gave birth to the Uncle Bob Test. He basically said that he did not want his friends and family in the business because he didn't want any "weirdness" down the road.

  At the time this sort of made sense, as bringing family into a risky business could make holiday dinners a bit awkward. But the more I pondered this fact, the more it bothered me. How would making your family and friends a great return on their money make things awkward?

The bottom line is this: Starting a company and wildly succeeding is one of the hardest things on earth to accomplish. As investors, we know that some of our investments will go bad, but we are looking for entrepreneurs who know beyond a doubt that they will succeed. We are looking for a special and resilient kind of person who absolutely refuses to fail.

The *Uncle Bob Test* is about having skin in the game. As investors, we want to see what the entrepreneur will lose if things go bad. When things get tough, and they will, losing strangers' money is one thing. Losing your own money is another thing, but losing your friends' and family members' money (your Uncle Bob's money) is something no one wants to do. This might sound intense, but it absolutely puts the entrepreneur on the same page with the investor – wanting and almost needing that exit strategy to happen sooner rather than later.

So just ask: Do you have any friends and family as investors? Ask them how much money they have in the deal and what percentage they currently own of the company. Ask if you can meet them or talk with them over the phone.

Salary Cap Test

I have already shared the story of the CEO who took $200K in salary while the company went south and the investors lost everything. No doubt the CEO of this company and the investors were not operating under the Same Page Philosophy.

The point of the entrepreneur being on a salary cap is not that we don't want to see the entrepreneur achieve wealth. We do want them to get wealthy – crazy wealthy, in fact, but we want them to get wealthy the same way as the shareholders. We want them to have a real want, almost a *need*, to follow through on the proposed exit strategy. As a reminder, there are only four ways for you to get an actual return on your investment:

1. Selling the company
2. Dividends
3. The company or a person buying your shares from you
4. Taking the company public

Without a salary cap for the founder, there is little incentive and certainly no urgency to execute the exit strategy. Unfortunately for me, I have learned the hard way and have a good bit of money that has been tied up in companies for over 10 years with founders that are doing just fine; they have no compelling reason to perform on their original exit strategy.

This can be a touchy subject to bring up, but if you explain why you are asking, any entrepreneur who understands the Same Page Philosophy will understand the importance of the topic.

One question in your mind might be, "what is the proper amount for a salary cap?" There is no magic number, but my goal has always been a number that pays the bills, but not much more than that. You don't want the founder to starve, but you want them hungry for the exit. If the founder has a strong need for more money on a regular basis, then encourage them to set themselves up on commission structures and/or bonuses for hitting objectives that move us toward the exit. Having the entrepreneur financially motivated to sell and/or hit profit numbers that moves the company closer to an exit can solve the cash flow needs of the entrepreneur and at the same time keep the Same Page Philosophy intact.

I usually approach the subject first by talking about the Same Page Philosophy and sharing the fact that I look for investments that encourage the founder to get wealthy the same way the shareholders will get wealthy. After discussing this, I can then approach the idea of a salary cap in a way that makes sense.

<u>One Driver Test</u>

Be leery of co-leaders. Best friends often start companies together, and although this is not necessarily negative, it's important to know where the final buck stops. Allow me to share an actual experience where I turned down an investment because it failed the One Driver Test:

- *I was very close to investing in this business. It was a real estate venture and I understood the business well. I had connections that would help, and all signs were leading me toward making this investment.*

  I knew the two founders were good friends and I knew they had different roles, but I wasn't quite sure about who was in charge. Which one of these guys was the one that would stay up until the wee hours solving problems and taking it for the team time and time again?

  What they told me was that both of them would stick it out. Both would work their fingers to the bone to make

> *it happen. But behind these claims, I saw an organizational chart without a head. Neither of them was willing to call the shots without the other. Neither was willing to report to the other. Neither was willing to take 100% responsibility for success or failure. This was a red flag. From my experience, it takes one driver. One person that cannot and will not fail. That one driver who naturally feels so much internal pressure to succeed that they will literally work 80-plus hours a week attacking problems, finding solutions and making it work.*

You may be thinking, "two heads are better than one, so why is the 'one driver' thing so important?" I do think two heads (and even three or four heads) are better than one when it comes to brainstorming, guiding, voting and other important pieces of the puzzle. But when it comes to asking yourself whether this is a good investment or not, having two drivers is an inherent flaw. What happens when one of them naturally works harder than the other? What happens when one of them has more of their friends' and family's money in the deal than the other? What happens when their skill sets overlap, or one person is not respected as much by the team as their counterpart? What happens if one of them falls in love, gets married and decides that "a balanced life" is more important than this particular business?

So many things can go sour between the two drivers. At one point, one or both will wonder whether or not it's worth it. Sure, one might rise above and become the one driver, but there are many pitfalls even in this instance.

Why should one of them rise to the leadership role if they each own roughly the same amount of equity? Will one of them have it in them to take a back seat? Sell or reduce their equity position? When there is a divorce, one never knows how ugly it can get until it happens.

The final meeting with the two sharply dressed friends gave me reason not to invest. They had failed the One Driver Test.

Administering this test is as simple as asking to see the organizational chart, usually called the "org chart." If they do not have one, ask them to describe what it will look like with the current team and what it might look like after the company grows significantly. You are not necessarily looking for a rigid org chart, but make sure there is one person who can handle the magnitude of both the responsibility and 24/7 mental commitment involved. And that same person should reap the lion's share of the reward if things go well.

Willing and Able to Sell Test

It's my belief that the founder is always the best salesperson for the company. Selling is difficult and often something the founder wants to outsource as soon as possible. I understand this and agree that it's important to begin building a sales team right away. However, I absolutely believe that one of the best things that the founder can do with 10 to 15 hours a week is to sell. The objection that I usually hear to this idea is: "I don't have time with all the other things on my plate," or, "I am not cut out for sales." All of this might be true; however, if you find an entrepreneur who is willing to keep sales as part of their weekly schedule, I believe it will do wonders for your investment.

First, it keeps the entrepreneur on the front line for part of the day, getting real insight to the many customer and market challenges that would not be visible to a leader who is always in the back office.

Second, the team will respect their willingness to get out there and swing the bat with the sales people.

Third, most likely they will be the best salesman in the company, even if they don't think of themselves as salespeople at first. The business card that says, "Founder," "President" or "CEO" will help open doors, plus they know the product or service better than anyone. Your CEO should naturally want to succeed more than anyone. This is a great sales asset.

If time is the main issue, I would much rather see the founder hire an assistant, or even two assistants, to handle details that would free them up for more selling rather than hiring extra salespeople while handling the details themselves.

Asking questions similar to this will help you discover the entrepreneur's intentions regarding selling:

1. How much time do you spend actually selling your product?
2. Are you planning on continuing doing sales yourself? If so, how much time will you commit to selling?
3. Tell me about your sales experience. Describe your sales style and philosophy.

4. Describe your follow-up process.
5. Selling is hard; tell me about times you have pushed through something where most people would have quit.

Product/Customer Test

Finding out the founder's view on product and customers is paramount. You're looking for someone who believes they are changing the world in some way – someone who believes their product solves a real problem. You're looking for someone who wants to help people and give them something amazing in exchange for their money. You are looking for someone who puts the customers first and who lives by the old saying, "the customer is always right." You want to see policies that ensure customer satisfaction.

I remember asking an entrepreneur some product/customer questions a few years ago. It went something like this: "Tell me what you love about your product and price point, and how you are helping your customer."

His answer went something like this: "That is what is so great about our margins. We are charging way more than what the product should sell for, but by the time the customer figures it out, we will have already made a ton of money."

This was a great way to short-term profit, but didn't sound workable in the long run. In my opinion, this sort of product/customer philosophy will always end badly. Even if you could make some quick money off the backs of uneducated customers, is this the kind of business you want to engage with? There's nothing wrong with commanding a premium price and earning a big margin, but a business based around "fooling" customers is an "avoid" scenario to me. I like to hear from an entrepreneur that they believe in their product enough to sell it to one of their own family members.

Here are a few questions that will help you discover how the entrepreneur feels about their product and customers:

1. Do you use the product yourself? Tell me about your friends' and family's experience with the product.
2. Do you have any testimonials for your product? Any complaints?
3. Tell me about your price point and how you feel you are helping your customers.
4. Do you feel that your product is life changing in any way?
5. Tell me about your customer policy regarding complaints, problems or returns.
6. Is there something emotional about your product that makes it exciting?
7. What is your plan for customer service, customer retention and customer satisfaction?

<u>Distraction Factor Test</u>

By now you should understand that starting and succeeding at a startup is *crazy hard.* It takes someone willing to wake up thinking about the company and go to bed thinking about the company. It takes dedication that might resemble someone preparing for the Olympics.

The Distraction Factor Test is simply making sure the founder is free from things that would detract from the laser focus they need. I would be cautious, for example, investing in a person who is a single parent of three young kids. I am not saying that a parent will not succeed at a startup, but if the entrepreneur is single with full custody and responsible for three young kids, it would be very difficult to maintain the focus required to succeed at a startup. The kids would naturally and properly take precedence over inevitable company crises. As an investor, you want to make sure that the entrepreneur has nothing major on their plate except the company. Some questions to ask:

1. Tell me about your personal life. Are you married? Kids? Girlfriend or boyfriend?
2. What other responsibilities are on your plate other than running this company?
3. Do you own a home or do you rent?
4. What other endeavors are you involved with? How much time do these take?
5. Tell me what you think your schedule will look like as you launch and run this company.
6. Is your family prepared for the dedication it takes to start and succeed at something like this? Tell me about how you have prepared them.

Leader Test

One of the most important concepts to remember is this: *It takes a team to build a sizable company and it takes a great leader to build a team.* It's just common sense; one person alone cannot grow a company to any size that will make investors wealthy. You are looking for an entrepreneur who has the understanding and skill set to build a team, to build a culture. You are looking for an entrepreneur who is a natural leader.

People follow leaders. Leaders then take those followers and create leaders out of them. Leaders lead by example. Leaders are transparent. Leaders empower their teams' creativity and work ethic. Leaders understand that ultimate responsibility belongs with them, yet the credit belongs to the team.

So how can you determine if this entrepreneur is a leader? Probing into their past a little bit will help, but also be very aware of the team they might have already started to build. Below are a few questions that will help you navigate this important test.

1. Tell me about your past; how did you become an entrepreneur?
2. Have you ever built and led a team for a common goal? Tell me about that. What is your philosophy regarding building a team?
3. Do you have a team started for this venture yet? Who is on the team? What are their skill sets? Would you be OK introducing me to a few of the people on your team?
4. How would you describe your leadership style?
5. What is your plan for building a team of key employees?
6. What is your plan for building a company culture? Do you have a mission statement?

7. What are your personal/business strengths and weaknesses? How do you plan on maximizing your strengths and overcoming your weaknesses?

Before we end this *Vetting the Entrepreneur* chapter, I will leave you with some general thoughts and questions that didn't fit nicely under one of the *tests*. These may help you frame your inquiry:

1. How transparent is this entrepreneur? Does it feel like the "poker game" or the "marriage?"
2. Do you get the sense that this entrepreneur will enjoy making others wealthy? (This is an important element of your assessment of the entrepreneur's character.)
3. Is this entrepreneur teachable or do they feel they "know everything?"
4. How does the entrepreneur plan on communicating with the investors? What is their personal goal with investors?
5. Has the entrepreneur had any conflict with business partners, investors or lenders before? Find out how things got resolved.
6. Have they ever had investors before? How did it work out for them? Are they OK with you meeting or talking with a few of them?

<u>Summary</u>

Vetting the entrepreneur is the most important and probably the most difficult part of your job as an investor. No entrepreneur will pass all these tests perfectly — please understand that these are really no more than guidelines to help you discover for yourself how you feel about the particular entrepreneur you are vetting.

Find an entrepreneur who is:

1. Totally transparent
2. Takes full responsibility
3. Willing to sell
4. Free from distraction
5. Willing to put family skin in the game
6. Willing to cap their salary
7. A natural leader who can build a team and puts themselves on the same page as the investor
8. Willing to cement promises into the Operating Agreement or Bylaws (which I will discuss at the end of the next chapter)

Having these qualities is no guarantee — but it will give you the solid foundation you are looking for.

Chapter Eight

Vetting the Team

Once you have established that the entrepreneur is a leader and, in fact, *The* Leader, it's important that you evaluate their team. The tests in this chapter are about the dynamics of the team, the structure of the business surrounding the team and a few motivational and financial factors that affect the team. As stated before: It's the team that builds a great company.

Multiple Personality Test

This test is about the handful of key team members: The leader's right and left hands.

- *A friend of mine once told me about a guest speaker at one of his MBA classes at Georgia Tech, and it has served me as a sort of guide ever since — and made me laugh. The speaker said this: "It takes three kinds of people to start and run a successful business. It takes a Visionary, a Detail Person and a Son of a Bitch."*

These attributes may be inside one person, but more than likely it takes two, three or even four people to create this magic. Either way, it's important to find out whether these attributes are a part of the core team. Let me explain.

The Visionary is the person who sees the future. They see the trends and can't stop brainstorming the next thing that will help take the company to the next level. This is the person who sees how fast the business world is changing and understands that the company must use technology to create strategies and processes that keep the company ahead of the curve. This person is often great with people, can build a culture and create excitement. Very important indeed, but without the Son of a Bitch and the Detail Person, this person will be an unsuccessful serial entrepreneur at best.

The Detail Person manages by the numbers. They are operators. They are implementers. They cross every "t" and dot every "i." They know the costs of everything and think in terms of margins, cash flow and profit. This is the person who can implement the systems and marketing that the Visionary sees. This person is a must in a successful venture, but without the Visionary and the Son of a Bitch, they will most likely not be able to build that crucial team culture, see into the company's future or keep believing even when the numbers just don't add up.

The Son of a Bitch is the person who will not quit – ever. They stand up and fight for the customer, for the quality of the product, for the shareholders. They are relentless and determined. They have a huge purpose and pick their fights carefully. This person often makes for long board meetings and can drive everyone crazy at times, but without them, success will most likely not happen.

Often the entrepreneur has, at some level, all of these traits, but usually dominates in one or two of them. Your job is to make sure that each of these traits is present across the core team. Sometimes I simply tell the story of the Georgia Tech speaker to help spur on a conversation and questions that help me determine whether I believe the team has what it takes to succeed. Once I share the funny story, most often the entrepreneur begins to shed light on the team and what each of them brings to the table. Below is an example of how to approach this topic and a few questions to also help you gather this information:

1. I once heard this story about a speaker who said, "it takes three types of people to start a business and succeed..." After explaining the three types briefly, then ask, "do you agree that it takes this mix of personalities and skill sets to succeed?"
2. Tell me which of the three personalities is dominant in you.
3. Tell me about your team and what traits they have. How long have they been with you? Have they invested money as well? How committed are they to the project?

Visionary Questions:

1. Tell me about the trends in this industry. Where do you think it's going and how does your vision synergize with current or future trends?
2. Tell me more about your plan for using technology to stay ahead of your competition.
3. Where do you see this company 10 years from now?
4. How would you navigate your way through another 2008 or other market recessions?
5. What would you do if this particular product/service does not take off?
6. Do you have an app in your future? If so, what will it do and how will it help?

Detail Person Questions:

1. Do you have financial statements for the past year that I could see?
2. I would love to see your *pro forma* for the next few years regarding costs, expenses, projected profit, etc.
3. Tell me about your operational and production processes and how you plan on implementing technology to create better systems over time.
4. Take me through the selling cycle of your product/service. Explain what happens with each lead depending on their level of interest.

Son of a Bitch Questions:

1. Tell me why you will not fail.
2. Tell me about a time in your life where you wanted to quit, you should have quit even, but for whatever reason you did not.
3. Why do you believe in this product/service?
4. Tell me where your company stands regarding "lowest price" strategy vs. "best quality" strategy. Show me how you plan on sticking with that strategy.
5. How do you plan on sticking with your customer philosophy? How much power will your staff have in saying "yes" to customers' requests or fixing their complaints?

Democracy Test

This test took me a while to develop — hindsight is always 20/20. Looking back on my 22 years of investing in startups has taught me a great deal.

Allow me to return to my personal statistics. If you recall, I have invested in 39 companies; three homeruns and nine that have made me solid returns. Out of those 12 companies that have made me money, eight of the 12 had founders who owned less than 51%. And 100% of my homeruns had founders who owned less than 51%.

In other words, the companies who made me the most money functioned democratically; i.e., big decisions such as creating new product lines, leasing new office space, selling the company, paying dividends or raising salaries all had to be voted on by a board of directors, who were in turn voted in or out by the majority of the shareholders, which was not one person.

Looking at this the other way brings me to the same conclusion. I have invested in three companies where my money has been "stuck" for over 15 years without any sign of an exit. In all three companies, the founders own more than 51%. My obvious conclusion is that investing in a dictatorship is not a smart idea. If the CEO and founders own controlling interest in the company, their board is toothless — if they even *have* a board. All the decisions can be made with or without a vote; authentic checks and balances don't exist. Same Page Philosophy goes out the window.

This can be a sensitive topic, but it's a very important one to cover. You will inevitably have founders who are dead set against giving up control. I would personally pass on those opportunities. You will also have founders who understand the situation and are willing to move toward controlling less than 51%, but don't want to dilute themselves too fast because they know they will need future rounds of bigger money down the road. This is a legitimate concern, and there are several creative ways to create a democracy before the founder drops below 51% via the operating agreement and/or creating class A and class B shares with regard to voting.

In order to determine whether this opportunity passes the Democracy Test, you need to find out the percentage that everyone on the team owns so far and what percentage they are selling in this round of money-raising. Here are a few questions that will help you navigate this test:

6. Would you please share with me the cap table – the current equity ownership of every shareholder since the inception of the company? What percentage of the company are you selling in this current raise?
7. Are there any shares set aside for employees or for the board of directors?
8. Are all the shares voting shares or do you have two classes?
9. After the dilution of this money-raising round, do you know what the equity ownership will look like for you and everyone else?
10. At the end of all money-raising, what percentage do you hope to keep for yourself?
11. Do you plan on being the CEO for the life of the company? How would you feel someday if the board decides that someone else is best suited to take the company to the next level?

Board of Directors Test

This test is intimately connected with the Democracy Test, as the owners of the company ultimately control, by vote, who is on the board and how the board functions. The board, in turn, votes on all the important issues that directly affect the investors' ROI. The desired board is one that is knowledgeable, can give an outside perspective and is naturally on the same page with the shareholders.

Knowledge: Clearly, if a board is to help with the direction of the company, they must be relatively seasoned and knowledgeable. Ask about the background of the board members or the potential board members. Have they started and sold a company before? Have they been involved with other startups in a significant way? Are they experts in the area or category that this company finds itself? What does each of them specifically bring to the table?

Outside Perspective: A board should provide an outside perspective, help with bigger-picture strategies, give direction/advice and help keep the company focused on the mission statement. For these reasons, it's important that the majority of the board is not directly involved with the day-to-day work of the business. Just ask!

Same Page as Shareholders: The board votes on big decisions that will directly affect the shareholders' return on their investment. Things like dividends, selling the company or salary and bonus decisions are all in the board's purview. Therefore, it's important that the board is on the same page as the shareholders and is incentivized as shareholders. Often the larger investors sit on the board, which naturally supports the Same Page Philosophy. If there are non-shareholders invited to serve on the board, it's important that the incentive plan for these board members consists of stock options rather than hourly or fee-based plans.

Ask something like this: "So tell me about your board or your future board. How are they incentivized for spending time helping with the direction of the company?"

Employee Option Pool Test

The Same Page Philosophy, from my experience, should also apply to the key employees, and in some cases, to all employees. Employee option pools are a way that employees can become part owners of the company over time.

This puts the employees on the same page with both the founder and the investors, and does wonders for building a great team. A few real-life examples will help you understand the importance of this:

- *One of my earlier investments was with an entrepreneur who had a CFO background. He was a natural numbers guy, watching over the costs, the margins and the cash flow, all of which we investors love to see.*

  He did not have an employee option pool, and at the time none of us investors really thought too much about it. The employees had great packages, including solid salaries and health insurance. The sales guys were making great money through commissions and everyone enjoyed year-end bonuses that made Christmas shopping fun!

  The entrepreneur ran a tight ship and things went very well with our investment for years. Then 2008 rolled around, and things started to unravel. The company was actually set up to weather the economy, as it had many of its clients on service contracts that kept revenue coming in. The problem ended up being high turnover among the sales team and other key positions. Not being able to keep top-notch salespeople and not being able to keep other key employees during the hard times set the company back at least five years. It was painful to watch. It was even more painful to see our investment suffer unnecessarily.

Why did these top team members leave the company? As I see it, they left because they saw themselves as employees rather than owners. As employees, they had no real reason to stick out the hard times. There was no incentive to stay around. Their upside consisted of base salaries, commissions, end-of-year bonuses and health insurance. When commissions and bonuses took a hit, there was little reason not to shop around for other job offers. Would a stake in the company, through stock options, have incentivized them to help the company weather the downturn? My experience says that it would have.

- *It seemed that almost every company was struggling in those years between 2008 and 2010. They were tough times. Yet, another company in which I am currently invested managed to keep their entire team intact through the struggles. They got more efficient; they worked as a team and thought outside the box. They worked smarter, emerging stronger than before. How did this company keep its key members through the storm? They were all shareholders or were earning options to become shareholders. They had an "owner" mentality. They took pay cuts and pay delays*

> *together. They thought long-term rather than short-term. As shareholders or soon-to-be-shareholders, they believed that helping the company improve through adversity would be more rewarding than trying to find another job.*

In case I have not said this enough, it takes a team to build a startup from nothing to something great. One person, regardless of how smart or dynamic, cannot build something huge. Option pools, when set up correctly, help create that team. They create owners, and by extension, a "we" company culture. They give people a reason to work late, become problem solvers instead of problem finders, and soldier through the invariable tough times. This kind of loyalty gives the company a winning edge and therefore increases the odds of success. A few simple questions will help you get started on this important test:

1. Are there any shares or a specific percentage of the company set aside for future employees or key team members? Tell me about that.
2. Are these shares voting shares? What percentage do these shares represent?
3. How do the employees vest into these shares?

<u>Lean Org Chart Test</u>

While you are looking at the org chart, it's important to find out if this entrepreneur understands how important it is to keep expenses low and to have everyone in the org chart doing the essentials – in other words, is their org chart lean or fat?

One mistake many entrepreneurs make is trying to grow the company with employees and managers, hoping that these hires will bring in sales rather than having lots of sales be the reason to hire more employees and managers. You can steer clear of this pitfall by asking some key questions about the leanness of the team:

1. Can you tell me about the roles of each of these people on the team?
2. How is each role critical to the success of the venture? What can you not achieve without person X, Y or Z?
3. How many managers are there at this point? Are the managers also selling? How is everyone compensated?
4. How does their pay compare to the pay of the same role in an established company?
5. Is anyone on a bonus program or any other incentive program?

Use of Funds Test

The Use of Funds Test is closely related to the Lean Org Chart Test: It's about how smart and strategic an entrepreneur will be in handling newly invested money. One of the best things to look for? Your money going toward things that are essential for building a foundation and scaling.

A classic idea coined by Michael E. Gerber in his book, *The E-Myth*, is that every company should *build systems as if they are going to franchise the business.* Whether franchising is the goal or not, creating systems that can scale is essential to the success of the venture.

Therefore, when you examine what the money invested is being used for, look for a good portion of the invested money to back foundational things like technology — software and hardware that will create the foundation needed for real growth. Securing a patent might be good use of funds. Inventory might also be a good use of funds, if the demand for the product or service is evident.

Red flags: The new money is going toward high salaries, high rent for a fancy office, unnecessary manager salaries or anything else that is not absolutely essential to the bottom line.

According to corporate legend, Elon Musk, founder of Tesla Motors and SpaceX, was asked for a raise by his longtime personal assistant. Musk suggested a vacation instead so he could see whether or not she was essential. She never returned to the position. Moral of the story: If money is going to something that the business can do without, it's not a good use of funds.

Below are a few questions that will help you open the conversation around use of funds:

1. What are your general plans for using the money being raised?
2. Tell me how your company will have better systems because of the money being raised.
3. What percent of the money raised will go toward inventory? Can you show me evidence of major demand for the inventory?

4. Can you show me that 100% of the money is going toward essentials? Can you demonstrate that every seat on the org chart is absolutely critical?
5. How will the money raised help you scale the company?

Operating Agreement/Bylaws Test

I mention this test toward the end for a reason. I have a dumb question: Have you ever had people promise you something that never actually happened? Of course you have. All of us have experienced this frustration in life. Someone makes a promise, even a handshake, and then for some reason, years later, it seems that each party remembers things differently.

Getting things in writing serves to protect friendships, protect business partnerships, and most important for our purposes, protect your investment.

For clarity I should mention that an Operating Agreement (OA) and Bylaws are essentially the same thing. Both are the official document that governs the rules, provisions and decision powers of the company. Operating Agreements are used with LLCs and S-corps and are signed by all the members, and Bylaws are used by C-corps and signed by their board of directors.

Most of the time, the OA or Bylaws are written by an attorney and written to protect the person who hired the attorney – the entrepreneur. Therefore, you will most likely not see any of these "tests" especially any "promises to fulfill these tests" in the typical OA or Bylaws. This might seem sad, but it's normal when you think of who hired the attorney and what their primary job is – to protect the entrepreneur. Why would an entrepreneur's lawyer, for example, encourage them to commit to a low salary in the OA? Or encourage their client's commitment to giving up control on certain decisions? Lawyers are primarily hired to protect their clients; typically, they are not entrepreneurs themselves and usually don't stand in the shoes of the investors.

All that said, you have a sales job ahead of you to get things in writing. It's not a hard sale, but a sale, nevertheless. Many of these tests don't need to be in the OA or Bylaws such as the *Uncle Bob Test* or the *One Driver Test.* These things will show up (or not) in the cap table and in the org chart. Certain tests, however, such as the *Democracy Test,* the *Salary Cap Test,* the *Board of Directors Test* and the *Employee Option Pool Test* can be and, I think, should be committed in writing.

In my humble opinion, if someone is willing to promise specifics in these areas (which is often one of the important reasons I feel comfortable investing) why wouldn't they be willing to commit to them in the OA? The Same Page Philosophy is a good thing when verbalized; it's a great thing when cemented in writing!

I encourage you to not get bogged down with this Operating Agreement/Bylaw task. Simply encourage them to commit in writing what they have already promised you. It can be as easy as adding a section in the OA or Bylaws titled Miscellaneous Provisions listing items such as salary caps, paying dividends to cover taxes and other promises made that can't be changed without requiring a super-majority (which can be 67% or 89% or whatever's needed) of the shareholders votes, therefore, giving the investors some control over these specific promises.

Summary

As stated many times before, the leader must build a team. The team is what builds a great company. Therefore it's paramount to understand the dynamics of the team. Look for teams that include not only a *Visionary*, but also a *Detail Person* and an *SOB* – someone who is relentless in their pursuit of both good values and success.

Stay away from companies where one person plans on having controlling interest. Find companies who have an experienced board of directors and an employee option pool so that the key team has an "owner" mentality. Look for a lean organizational chart and a specific and smart use of funds. And don't forget to ask the entrepreneur to walk their talk so to speak, by adding those specific promises they have made into their Operating Agreement or Bylaws.

Chapter Nine

Where are all these Opportunities?

Where do we find these opportunities? Are there "good" and "bad" places to find startup opportunities? First of all, let's assume that the readers here aren't planning to go toe-to-toe with the Silicon Valley venture capital folks. In the US, business media is obsessed with big, disruptive ideas, billion-dollar valuations and the Next Big Thing.

But don't get tunnel vision here: You don't have to have the next Google or Twitter in the works to deliver a good return on your investment. You might find a really good opportunity in a more traditional or underserved sector: Maybe an entrepreneur near you has an idea for serving a traditional need in a new region or has found a way to dominate the car wash market in a given ZIP code. It's not always about disruptive and sexy technology! That's why my portfolio includes investments in all sorts of categories. With a focus on the entrepreneur rather than the type of company, you can remain open to all ideas.

Here are a few "starter kit" ideas for finding opportunities:

- First, you will be pleasantly surprised by how powerful word of mouth is. Get some business cards made that say *Startup Investor* or *Angel Investor* and start telling people that one of the things you do is invest in startup companies. People will come out of the woodwork, so to speak, with an uncle or a neighbor who is starting a company and would love to have coffee with you. I think this is the best place to find opportunities. The reason for this is simple: It's a real "non-stranger" connection, and you will be better able to judge the character of the entrepreneur face to face, which is the most important piece of the puzzle.
- "Crowdfunding" has become a buzzword in the startup world. Kickstarter.com is one of the original sites, but many more have popped up over the past several years. Most of these are set up for the entrepreneur to help them raise money, but not by the traditional angel investor model. Much of the money raised is in the form of donations, but this niche is quickly growing into a great source

for investors big and small. This is a great way to see what kind of ideas are bubbling up from the ground level and to gauge how entrepreneurs and creatives are claiming to deliver on their ideas.

- Meetups, clubs and local events that focus on innovation and business groups are a no-nonsense starting point for making the rounds, getting your name out there and identifying potential stars of your local entrepreneurial community. I've noticed Startup Weekend events popping up all over the United States. Get these and similar events on your radar.
- Joining an investment club can be the surest way to meet your objectives of finding and investing in 10 startups. Investment clubs leverage the minds of others and can help reduce the risk significantly. If there isn't one in your area, start one!
- Mine your relationships: Former colleagues and clients, alumni groups or industry networks are great places to put out your feelers. I got a big boost from my fraternal connection with the book-selling company, Southwestern — the company where I got my start in business.

There's no "perfect" way to start. It only matters that you get started. As I learned back in my book-selling days: Now is the time!

Would you like to be notified of startup opportunities from entrepreneurs who have read Todd's material?

We are envisioning *The Everyday Startup Accelerator*, where Everyday Investors virtually meet Everyday Entrepreneurs.

Jump on the waiting list at:

www.theeverydaystartupaccelerator.com

Our Pledge and Promise:

- NEVER an OBLIGATION to Invest, EVER.
- FREE to sign up.
- NO Junk Mail
- We will NEVER Give or Sell Your Email to anyone.
- Easy to Find "UNSUBSCRIBE" Button if you ever want to be removed from the list.

Chapter Ten

Breaking it Down to a Cheat Sheet

Rules of Thumb Before Investing

1. You should turn down at least four out of every five you analyze.
2. Invest in 10 or none at all.
3. Be willing to lose every dime you invest in startups.
4. Don't invest based on emotion – professional help with analysis is recommended.
5. Find a devil's advocate to help you stay logical in your decision.
6. Consult your attorney before investing and if you are unaccredited, follow all the rules of the Jobs Act.

Tips for Successful Q&As

Avoid yes/no questions; rather, ask open-ended questions, such as, "how do you plan on communicating to your investors?"

After you get an answer to a question, try to follow up with, "tell me more about this or that."

Sometimes the most relevant information comes indirectly. Listen for topics and clues you can follow up with more questions. Follow these rabbit trails as deep as they naturally go.

The Quick Checklist

1. The Idea
    b. Do you truly understand it?
    c. Has it been tested?
    d. What trends impact the idea?
    e. Can it scale?
    f. Does the entrepreneur have a handle on sales, marketing, technology and systems?
2. The Offering and The Exit
    c. Is the valuation fair?
    d. Any sweeteners offered?
    e. What's the projected ROI? (Cut it in half, double the time.)
    f. Is The Exit plan detailed and realistic?
3. The Entrepreneur (Character and Skill Set)
    d. Uncle Bob Test
    e. Salary Cap Test
    f. One Driver Test
    g. Willing to Sell Test
    h. Product/Customer Test
    i. Distraction Factor Test
    j. Leader Test

4. The Team
    e. Multiple Personality Test
    f. Democracy Test
    g. Board of Directors Test
    h. Employee Option Pool Test
    i. Lean Org Chart Test
    j. Use of Funds Test
    k. Operating Agreement/Bylaws Test

Afterword
A Perspective on Wealth

Making a million dollars, losing a million dollars, and then making it back does weird things to the psyche. It certainly puts money in perspective. I have always known money doesn't make people happy, but going through the ups and downs with money certainly solidified this truth. Some of the happiest times of my life were before the first million and after its loss. Not that I have not had happy times having money, but it was never money that was the source of the joy.

So why create wealth? I urge you not to make the mistake of striving for wealth thinking it will make you happy — or even happier. You will be extremely disappointed, at best. Wealth from my perspective is a path to freedom. Freedom gives you time. Time for what? To be present with people, to follow your passions, to give back, to create, to travel, to be a better parent, partner or sibling. Money is a tool, no more and no less.

We have all heard the truth: "You can't take it with you." If you have had a close friend or family member die, you know this truth all too well. It's a strange thing to witness, and a hard way to learn, but once you know this truth, it can be invigorating. Are we owners or stewards? Owners or managers? We might think we own our money, business assets, real estate, or toys, but if it's true that "you can't take it with you," then isn't it truer that we are mere stewards or managers of our stuff?

Thinking of myself as a manager of whatever money or asset I happen to have in my possession, rather than the owner, has been a nice paradigm shift. This truth has allowed me to grow the nest egg without getting attached to it. It allows for losses and wins to pass through me as lessons learned. It's a refreshing truth that actually puts all of investing in perspective.

Lastly, I thank you for your investment of time in reading these words. I wish you all the best as you venture out into the startup world.

Todd E. McWhirter

Acknowledgements

I have always looked forward to this part of the writing a book... The thankful part.

Writing does not come natural for me; therefore, I have many people to thank. My mother, a retired teacher, read each book multiple times finding and correcting grammar errors. More importantly, she kept believing in me. Thank you, Mom!! My Dad, from early on, helped me understand money- both how to save and how to think about it. Thank you, Dad! My girlfriend, Tammie, of 14 years stuck with me through my loss of everything. Thankfully she kept believing I would land on my feet. She's a goof ball - calls me Teeter Todder - and likes to say "teeter todders but he doesn't fall down". Thank you, Tammie, for believing in me! My kids, Ethan and Ellie, were huge supporters, asking me questions, interested in my progress, throwing their 2 cents in on cover choices, etc. They keep me motivated in so many ways it's hard to even quantify. Thank you, Ethan! Thank you, Ellie! A big thank you to Dave Ness, Doug Horch and Brian Grayson for encouraging and helping me early on, back when we were calling it the 50X project – great memories!

The book(s) would not be the same without Nate Warren and Durand Achée, my editors. So much time we all spent going over the details. Thank you Both! I wrote these pages by locking myself down at a coffee shop each morning, not leaving until I finished 3 hours of work. That place was *The Bike Café* in Denver Colorado. Thank you Jess and Peter for creating such a great atmosphere and welcoming me personally each morning for all that time. Without the amazing entrepreneurs and the loyal investors who came along side some of my good decisions and bad decisions, none of the content would have ever came to pass. Some are mentioned in the stories I tell, some are not, there are many and you know who you are. Thank you so very much! And finally, I want to thank all my friends and family who supported me in the process, voting on covers, giving thoughts on content, adding so much value and helping with those little things that as we know are the big things. There are many of you, and again, you know who you are. Sincerely, Thank you!!

About the Author

Following an impressive 14-year career in sales and sales management, **Todd E. McWhirter** transitioned into an Angel Investor almost by accident. He likes to call himself the "accidental startup investor", yet through his hands-on experience evaluating over 400 startups over the past 23 years, McWhirter has developed a proven and practical methodology that resulted in 39 startup investments that have generated a remarkable 7X overall return, growing his investment dollars from thousands to multi-millions.

Through years of comprehensive experience, including dramatic wins, bankruptcy and an amazing come back, McWhirter documented what worked and what did not. He turned these notes into two books: one for entrepreneurs looking to raise capital – *Funding Your Startup* – and one for everyday people, just like himself, to begin investing in startup companies – *The Everyday Startup Investor.*

More than anything, this accidental investor is a team player who wants to help everyone around him succeed. With the JOBS Act finally making it legal for non-accredited investors to participate in funding emerging growth companies, his passion to guide and support others in this exciting entrepreneurial adventure is expressed in these two books.

www.ingramcontent.com/pod-product-compliance
Lightning Source LLC
LaVergne TN
LVHW051011080826
845145LV00009B/2570